Edith Sitwell

MUSIC AND CEREMONIES

Edith Sitwell

Music and Ceremonies

THE VANGUARD PRESS, INC.
NEW YORK

IN MEMORY OF DAVID

only child of my cousins
Veronica and Frank Gilliat

Contents

Preface

From time to time, mainly in England, an outcry arises on the subject of the use of the arts in general, and of poetry in particular. This seems to me very odd. Who was it bade us "Consider the lilies of the field"? Why should everything in the world, necessarily, be of use? And what do we mean when we speak of *use*? Although poetry has, or should have, the beauty of the lily, it is as unseeing to ask what is the *use* of poetry as it would be to ask what is the use of religion.

As that great writer Jean Cocteau said: "The spirit of poetry is indeed the religious spirit outside all precise religion."

"He from the sunlike centrality and reach of his vision," said Emerson of Plato, "had a faith without cloud."

This was always true of the great poet. It was true in the past, and is true in this age, when so many human beings, because of the outer circumstances of the world and their lives, suffer from a tragic weakening or total loss of faith. Poetry helps to keep us in that sunlike centrality.

The poems in this book are those written since the publication of my *Collected Poems* and will eventually form a part of my collected work.

Much of my life has been spent in studying what other poets and artists in the other arts have written about technical necessities. Therefore, all the prefaces I have written are full of these. Since the publication of my *Collected Poems* I have moved, technically, in different ways.

In *Façade,* for instance, the poems often "warmed themselves at fantastical fires and danced in the light of glow-worms," as Thomas Campion said in one of his prefaces. But I remembered that "Poetry should always be running on pleasant feet, sometimes swift, sometimes slow." [1]

Now I am an old woman, I remember these lessons learned in my early days.

[1] Puttenham, *Art of English Poesy,* 1589.

I need hardly say that I am not comparing myself with Dryden, Pope, or Donne; but it is not out of order to remember what Coleridge wrote of these three great poets: "To read Dryden, Pope, etc., you need only count syllables, but to read Donne you must measure Time and discover the Time of each word by the sense of passion."

During the last ten years or so, there has been a general attempt on the part of incompetent versifiers to remove all grandeur from poetry, to flatten it down into the lifelessness of the lesser Victorian verse. Reading the nonsense these people produce, I remember a phrase from No. 6 of Jeremy Taylor's *Twenty-five Sermons:* "A man of ordinary piety is like Gideon's Fleece, wet in its own locks, but it could not water a poor man's garden."

But the poor man's garden should, surely, be considered.

If certain critics and poetasters had their way, "Ordinary Piety" and its child, Dullness, would be the masters of poetry.

Robert Browning, a fine but flawed poet, has been held responsible by some of these critics for the wrong tendencies held today in certain quarters. But he is treasured by them for his flaws, not for his virtues.

Father Gerard Manley Hopkins, in a letter to R. W. Dixon, said: "Browning has, I think, many frigidities. Any untruth to nature, to human nature, is frigid. Now he has got a great deal of what came in with Kingsley and the Broad Church School, a way of talking and making his people talk, with the air and spirit of a man bouncing up from the table with a mouth full of bread and cheese, and saying that he meant to stand no damned nonsense."

This is, I think, a very fair description of some of Browning's inferior work.

We have, at this time, a good deal too much of the Broad Church School in poetry. And the Broad Church School boys cling together, reminding me strongly of interludes in one of the late Miss Nellie Wallace's songs, in which, removing her hat, she would implore the two frondless feathers that decorated it, "For God's sake, hold together, boys!"

There is a good deal of yapping and snapping about "usefulness." Mr. F. W. Bateson, in a book called *English Poetry,* declared: "Poetry is only useful in the sense that it is not self-regarding, a disinterested activity. In its essence it is simply a part, in some respects a culmination, of the process of social living, one of those things like law-abidingness, and politeness, voting at a General Election, or reading the newspaper, that life in a human community necessarily involves."

Well, you can't say fairer than that, can you? But poets see poetry from a different point of view. In one of the most important books of criticism written in our time, M. Marcel Raymond said: *"Ce n'est pas question de capter à sa source la vie immédiate, en sa matérialité brute, mais d'élucider toutes choses, de leur restituer leur signification authentique."*

I do not mean—I have never meant—that we must avoid the everyday world. Reason and tranquillity were the companion angels of Wordsworth as he walked through our everyday world made splendid by the light of a genius that illuminated but did not transform. Common speech and common experience were there, but all made radiant and unforgettable by inspiration.

There were days—the "Intimations of Immortality from Early Childhood" was such a day—when the Pentecostal Flames came, for a moment, to our common speech. The ordinary objects of life became supernatural. The common celandine was still the common celandine, but it was also a star. For Wordsworth had the warmth of the earth and of the human heart; and that genius which was rather of the heart than of the soul had taken all the chill from Reason.

'The earth and every common sight
To me did seem
Apparelled in celestial light.'

Poetry is, indeed, the deification of reality, and one of its purposes, among others, is to show that the dimensions of man are, as Sir Arthur Eddington said, "Halfway between those of an atom and a star."

E. S.

13

MUSIC AND CEREMONIES

The Outcasts

for Jean le Roy

And wi Oblivion's Kiss
Ye win.
        —SYDNEY GOODSIR SMITH

This is the night-moment when the Damned,
Rejected by pools that slake the thirst of beasts of prey,
Creep in the rags of their hearts to Judas. This,
The moment of the year
When comes a drop of mercy to those lips
That kissed but to betray.
"O brother, pity me!
One drop, only one drop!" No answer came.
They crept away
To their hell that is the Dead Sea shore. Their bliss,
Their love, they knew now was a Pillar of Salt,
From whom they had hoped to win Oblivion's Kiss.

March Past

In this August of the world, amidst the auguries
And auspices of whispering dust,
The increase of honor and of Dives' honey,
And the green seeds of predestination lying
Under the almond husk of what was once the world,
Young soldiers were marching, and so gay
They looked, their muskets bright as sparkles of the day
And the great heat, you could not tell the dark
Would overtake them. . . . Yet their shadows in the dust,
Under the great gold sun, were ragged, bent
And haggard, as though they were already old.
These foolish mockeries walked side by side
With the strong young men whose steady trained
March raised up the dust, until you knew
The whole world was but this. The trumpet's sound
Was the voice heard thrice before the first cock crew;
And in the heat the sound of marching feet
Intensified
Until you thought six million men were on the march
From the grave of the world, the town called Sarajevo.

The War Orphans

(Written after seeing a photograph of Korean children asleep in the snow.)

The snow is the blood of these poor Dead . . . they have no
    other—
These children, old in the dog's scale of years, too old
For the hopeless breast—ghosts for whom there is none to
    care,
Grown fleshless as the skeleton
Of Adam, they have known
More aeons of the cold than he endured
In the first grave of the world. They have, for bed,
The paving stones, the spider spins their blankets, and their
    bread
Is the shred and crumb of dead Chance. In this epoch of the
    cold,
In which new worlds are formed, new glaciations
To overcast the world that was the heart,
There is only that architecture of the winter, the huge plan
Of the lasting skeleton, built from the hunger of Man,
Constructed for hunger—piteous in its griefs, the humiliation
Of outworn flesh, the Ape-cerement, O the foolish tattered
    clothing,
Rags stained with the filth of humanity, stink of its toiling,
But never the smell of the heart, with its warmth, its fevers,
Rapacity, and grandeur. For the cold is zero
In infinite intensity, brother to democratic
Death, our one equality, who holds
Alike the maelstrom of the blood, the world's incendiarism,
The summer redness and the hope of the rose,
The beast, and man's superiority o'er the beast
That is but this:
Man bites with his smile and poisons with his kiss.
When, in each dawn,
The light on my brow is changed to the mark of Cain,

And my blood cries, "Am I my brother's keeper?" seeing these
    ghosts
Of Man's forgetfulness of Man, I feel again
The pitiless but healing rain—who thought I only
Had the lonely Lethe flood for tears.

to L. P. Hartley

1   The Death of Prometheus

Outside the wall
Of the death-room where the tall
Prometheus lay,
As gray as a boxing kangaroo Eternity's sea is fighting
A yawning ghost—a ghost with a donkey's bray:
"Hee-haw!
See-saw!
Now up, now down,
Now King, now Clown!
I am the new Equality, mine is the day."
No Furies watch, for in their place are flies
Who with the beating of dark wings are finding
The world's new rhythm (a little buzzing in air, then silence),
In which the Giant and Dwarf take it in turns
To rule: Up Giant! Down Dwarf! Up Dwarf!
Down Giant! Thin as Man's faith, or the Writing on the
     Wall,
The teachers laugh (Jim No-one, small Joe None,
Jack Straw and John Raw),
And Man is alone.
"Not much of a world to leave!" Prometheus said.
Then, as world-long he lay on his death-bed,
With the marrow of his bone, his brain, clean-eaten
By those who were his friends, the great fires beaten
To ash from the Burning Bush that was his heart,
His Will was read to those friends. No deserts hold
Beasts more desperate [1]—horses pretending to be men,
And riding men for horses, foxes, jackals,
Hiding behind their human faces. Bold,

The little Jackal with his gilded pelt
(Hiding the leprous spot and the world's rot)
Giggles, "No more need I know the Lion's weather—
But a time to sprawl and to wear the Ape's feather!
I shall boast of the Lion's kill as my own,
And shall build my castle of the Lion's bone!"
And with that all the animals hell-howled together,
With yawning mouths like Time's, into whose maw
In the end all Caesars, cities, suns,
Will in their ruin fall
With old bacchantes of the suburbs and the red
Lilies named Cynorrhodon—yet more
Voracious. But the Giant's Will said,
"My loving friends, on my life you have richly fed.
But now you have eaten me bare to the heart and bone,
You must look to One you starved in your greed—
Not the see-saw world (there is no world left, all is loss).
There is only the echo that quenches the thirst in Hell—
The sound of the terrible tears that will fall from the Cross."

1   ". . . No deserts hold
Beasts more desperate. . . ."
        —MARTIN SCRIBBLERUS

2   At the Crossroads

The Beast of Prey has not a history—
A blaring backward shadow of despair
Or triumph—only the shadow of the Lion's paw
Across the world, foretelling the new Law.

In the month of mellow August, of the auguries
Of dust, and yellow moons and melons, shadows
Yellow as the ripeness and the wheat
Fall in the great heat
On crossroads of the world, where Man must make
The choice—of the backward road to the Peaceful Ape,
Or the forward road to the company of the Lion
That has no backward history, but only
The long predestination of the Lion's paw.

Where the crossroads meet, the toppling gods of straw,
Gapus, Vervactoris, Convectoris,
Imporcitoris (nodding at John Raw
and Niny-Nany: Man pretending to be real)
Whine "We are wheat" to the grave's mocking maw.
One creaks:
"Man follows our rocking law—
Changed by each hollow breeze." Convectoris said,
"Ripeness is all!

And Man's whole duty is to find the quickest way to fall.
You, King and Beggar, who in the womb wore the Ape's coat,
The lanugo, should learn in the Ape's school
To walk on all fours, cast a longer shade to cool
The world—you who are now but shade!" Another teacher
    said,

"If Man rejects the religion of the Straw,
The Lion will blot out History—The paw
Of the Lion who finds its nourishment in Man's bones

25

That have grown dry as the bones of Tantalus
From thirst of gold, this will erase
The scarlet dawns of History in the veins. . . .
Darkness is all."
So sounds the Fool's song, as he sees our planet cool.

Line 1 was inspired by a phrase by Professor Martin Buber.

Choric Song

for Elizabeth Salter

The Red Woman, like the glittering
Dark red cedar tree
Or the sun when its fires are low—
The Eskimo, black as the ancient cold, with her hair like the
    long dull ropes of snow
Let down from the creaking cloud—
The White Woman, the huge lightning in the dark of the great
    world—
The Negress black as thunder, the dead woman upright in the
    Spring's shroud—
They shout to their loves across the ocean, the glittering seas
    of delight—
"Mine is the only love in the world, the first beginning of
    sight!
Oh you, the hour when the work of the world, the hunt for our
    food, is done—
Love me, my ultimate Darkness, kiss me, my infinite Sun!"

Praise We Great Men

for Benjamin Britten

Praise we great men
From all the hearths and homes of men, from hives
Of honey-making lives.
Praise with our music those
Who bring the morning light
To the hearts of men, those households of high heaven. Praise

We those gods of sound
Who stole the frozen fire
From gilded hives upon Mount Parnassus,
(Hives gilded by the light)—compressed
That honey-red fire into holy forms
That emulate those of the hives of heaven. Praise

Those who can raise
Gold spirits of men from their rough Ape-dust, and who see
The glory, grandeur hidden in small forms:
The planetary system in the atom, and great suns
Hid in a speck of dust. Praise we the just—

Who are not come to judge, but bless
Immortal things in their poor mortal dress,

And ripen lives and rule our hearts and rhythms,
Immortal hungers in the veins and heart.

Praise be to those who sing
Green hymns of the great waters to the dry
And tearless deserts in the souls of men, until
Under the fertilization of their singing breath
Even the grayness and the dust of Death
Seem the gray pollen of the long September heat. O praise

With lion-music such as that heard in the air
When the roaring golden lion that roams the heavens
Devours the dark, and multitudes and magnitudes respond

To that lion-music. . . . And on wings
Of music let us rise
Like velvet honey-flies
To praise the gods of sound with those bee-murmurings:

The sound of violins
And the clear sound of flutes
As round as honeyed fruits—
(And like the water-Phoenix ever rising
For wanderers in the lonely desert sand—)

Praise we these earthly gods—
Praise with the trumpet's purple sound—
Praise with the trumpet flower
And with that flower the long five-petalled hand
That sweeps the strings.
Praise with that Angel of High God, the voice—
O let us still rejoice
And praise we these great men from the first hour
Of the spirit's birth until our earthly setting

Into the night of Death.
Praise with our last breath
These earthly Gods who bring
All sounds, all faiths, delights, and splendors lost
Beneath the winter's frost
Back to the hearts, the hearths and homes of men.

Fires on the hearth, fires in the skies, fires in the human heart,
Praise we great men!

"His Blood Colors My Cheek"

A saying of St. Agnes

for the Very Rev. M. C. D'Arcy, S.J., LL.D., D.Litt., Litt.D., F.R.S.L.

His Blood colors my cheek.
Ah! Were but those Flames the tongue wherewith I speak
Of the small ambitions I have seen
Rise in the common street
Where the bell that tolls in Bedlam tolls the hour.
Yet still great flowers like violet thunders break
In air, and still the flower of the five-petalled senses
Is surely ours.
I, an old dying woman, tied
To the winter's hopelessness
And to a wisp of bone
Clothed in the old world's outworn foolishness
—A poor Ape-cerement
With all its rags of songs, loves, rages, lusts, and flags of
    death,
Say this to you,
My father Pithecanthropus Erectus, your head once filled with
    primal night,
You who stood at last after the long centuries
Of the anguish of the bone
Reaching upward towards the loving, the all-understanding
    sun—
To you, who no more walk on all fours like the first
Gardener and grave-digger, yet are listening
Where, born from zero, little childish leaves and lives begin!
I hear from the dust the small ambitions rise.
The White Ant whispers: "Could I be Man's size,

"My cylinders would stretch three hundred feet
In air, and Man would look at me with different eyes!"

And there the Brazilian insect all day long
Challenges the heat with its heavy noise:
"Were I as great as Man, my puny voice
Would stretch from Pole to Pole, no other sound
Be audible. By this dictatorship the round
World would be challenged—from my uproar would a new
Civilization of the dust be born, the old world die like dew."
I watch the new world of rulers, the snub-nosed,[1] the vain and
    the four-handed,[2]
Building a new Babel for the weak
Who walk with the certainty of the somnambulist
Upon the tight-rope stretched over nothingness—
Holding a comet and the small Ape-dust in their fist
Over the grave where the heart of Man is laid.
I hear the empty straw whine to the street
Of the ghost that has no bread, the lonely ghost
That lacks prosperity: "I am your Wheat:
Come and be fed!"
But I see the sun, large as the journeying foot of Man, see the
    great traveller
Fearing no setting, going straight to his destination,
So am I not dismayed.

His Blood colors my cheek;—
No more eroded by the seas of the world's passions and
    greeds, I rise
As if I never had been Ape, to look in the compassionate, the
    all-seeing Eyes.

[1] "According to a statement of an ancient Chinese work of about 2000 B.C., a so-called man of the Hen Yeung Kingdom appears from his up-turned nose to be a snub-nosed monkey" (Rhinopithecus).—*Man as an Animal*. W. C. Osman Hill, M.D., F.R.S.E. (Hutchinson University Library).

[2] "At one time, it was indeed the practice, in spite of their recognised and obvious connection with man, for apes and monkeys to be called *Quadramana,* or four-handed ones (and) to relegate man to a separate order called *Bimania* (i.e., two-handed)."—*Op. cit.*

The Yellow Girl

for Alberto de Lacerda

In this island (Hispaniola) are certain glow wormes that shine in the night, as doe ours . . . but give a greater light, so much that when the men of the Iland goe any journeys in the night, they beare some of these wormes made fast about their feet and head, in such sort that he should see them afarre. By the light of these also, the women worke in their houses in the night.
— GONZALO DE ORVIEDO

Once the Reverend Thomas Glover,
In the prow of his boat drifting
O'er a sea as clear as tropic
Air, read from the Holy Book
By the light of a small worm.
(All the heavens and God's Fire
Revealed through a small worm's desire.)

A skeleton lying on the sand
(Like the gold-dark skeleton of the sun)
That ship-wrecked sailor sighing said:

"The leaf-dark King of Aragon
Sent me as Ambassador
To the Sultan of Great Babylon
Over the sea (a world of leaves)
But I was wrecked upon Time's sands
And in the isle of my Yellow Girl
I died of the Yellow Fever, O!

"For she was brighter than the gold
That falls from the leaves of Hispaniola;
A bouquet of the yellow stars,
Her mouth . . . Her voice like moonlight, **or**
The voice of the sea-sorrow, told
Me 'Wander not—I love thee!' So

I slept with that yellow moonlight, and
I died of the Yellow Fever, O!

"Some men turn skeletons for gold,
And some for love of the horizons;
Or because Truth, a water-lady
As inconstant as the wave,
Rose from the depths of the tropic sea
And lured them to her siren cave.
But at the last, all things are one:
Gold, Truth, and the skeleton of the sun
When we alone are lying.

"My girl was lovely as Idleness,
But Shadow now, the giantess,
(Dark Africa as calm as palm trees) is
My sole companion.
Grave sir, you preach with book and bell
Against the Yellow Girl, the moonlight
I had thought was day. . . .
And yet, despise not the poor clay:
Do you not read the Holy Book
By the despisèd small worm's light—
All the heavens and God's Fire,
All the Spirit's storm
Revealed through a small worm's desire?"

Song

Said the Bee to the Lion
"My life is a gold prayer—"
Said the laughing Sun
"My life is the gold air."

Said the Lion to the Bee
"My life is that of the Sun; in hot gold, I rage through the
    gold air."

But I who have known the weight of the August air
And the gold heat in the heart

Am like a bright small star in a starry sky
Bright to myself only.

A Girl's Song in Winter

for Cyril Connolly

That lovely dying white swan, the singing sun,
Will soon be gone. But seeing the snow falling, who could tell
    one
From the other? The snow, that swan-plumaged circling crea-
    ture, said,
"Young girl, soon the tracing of Time's bird-feet and the
    bird-feet of snow
Will be seen upon your smooth cheek. Oh, soon you will be
Colder, my sweet, than me!"

La Bella Bona Roba

for Harold Acton

I cannot tell who loves the skeleton
Of a poor marmoset, nought but boan, boan,
Give me a nakednesse with her cloaths on.
— RICHARD LOVELACE

Alas, lass, lost—
Alas, lost.

Where is my white velvet dress
Of flesh that some called heaven, some sin—
Not pitying the grave that is
Not slaked, that is not satisfied,
For all its triumph? Ah, lass, lost!
Alas, lost.

My arms were mighty as the seas
That gird the great young seeding lands
To make them theirs, and in my hands
Men's fortunes were as Time's sand in
The glass . . . I gave them at the last
The small red worm for paramour.
Where is that might now? Ah, lass, lost!
Alas, all lost.

Once my love had the lion's mouth,
My breasts were the pillars of the South.
Now my mouth has the desert's drouth,
And all that comes
To my breast is the wind and rain—
Alas, lass, lost,
Alas, lost.

The tigerish Spring was in each vein;
The glittering wind of Spring, my mane.

Now am I no more to Spring
Than the violet mist from vine-branches.
Alas, lass, lost.
All, lass, lost.

Now is my body only this:
The infinite geometry
That is the cold. How could I know
Winter would take me, I grow old?
Alas, lass, lost!
Alas, lost.

Young girl, you stare at me as if
I were that Medusa Time
That will change you, too, to stone:
So you, grown old, must lie alone.
Alas, lass, lost!
Alas. . . .

Prothalamium

for the Marriage of the Duke and Duchess of Kent,
8th June 1961

Now the great flower of the world
And its gold bee, the sun
With all its hives and lives of honeyed light
—The Queens and lilies born on British soil—
The Queens with eyelids like the young narcissus
Shall bless this youth and innocence—young people
Like the spring rainbows, risen from all growth,
The sap and singing, tall among the trees.

The music of the air, the flame of flowers
Are lustrous with their youth, like the first spring when it
    began
In the young world before the Fall of Man.

The white bride and the forest of white flowers
Upon the Altar, and white lightnings of the dew
(Each drop Altair and Sirius) fallen from the petals
Seem one. And like the music of the air,
The young children following—
The bridesmaids with their curls as blond as water.

                    Love is all life, the primal law,
The sun and planets to the husbandman,
The kernel and the sap; it is the power
That holds the Golden Rainers in the heavens, bringing us
The calyx of the flower of the world, the spirit
Moving upon the waters, the defeat
Of all time's ravages.
                    Upon this happy day—
Even for the old, whose winter was flowerless, whose bones
    are sunless

(Yet older than Spring), their winter breaks again in flower
Till summer grows from a long-shadowed kiss.

Who was it cried, "This is no time for sowing or begetting.
The East is yellow with fear, and the West is red with its
    setting"?

Although a gray bough drips
With dews of death, still the lost floras of the world
Lie on young cheeks, young lips.

Music and Ceremonies

To Charles and Kathleen Musk

The emerald lightnings of the snow are gone:
The fires that sealed the earth.
And green shoots of the first lilies pierce the ground
Stronger than those flames! The sound
Of these green violent thunders of the lilies' growth arises
From all the weight of earth, the centuries.

His face broad as the Scythian plains,
With slanting eyes
Like the green rainbows of the Spring,
The Man of Emeralds danced beneath the bough—
          Danced like a wave
Amid the thunders of the rising sap. . . .
Music and Ceremonies . . . these
Make the earth and heaven harmonize.

For dark are music's springs;
The ancient Kings
Drew them from the rising of the sap. . . .
          The grand Beginning of all things
From which all life arises. . . .
From Music and from Ceremonies grow
The harmony and benevolence of all that lies
Between the earth and the great flowering boughs of the spring
     skies.

All harmonies arise
From the great harmonies of the spring growth
Ruled by the heavens. . . . But in Ceremonies
We are ruled by earth
And its gradations, that divide
The greatest from the least . . .

43

The Beast and Plant, descending third and fifth of Man
In the great scale of Being . . . for the Plant
Is a Beast retarded by the Dark; the Beast,
A Plant grown free, that blossoms in the light
Devoid of root like the flowers in the air.

Music and Ceremonies keep
Green heaven high in air and the green earth
Beneath our dancing feet. . . .
Music and Ceremonies give the laws for planting
And budding, and the slanting
Of the first emerald rainbow of the Spring
And the green tender rain, said the Man of Emeralds
          Dancing underneath the bough.

Music is Heaven, Ceremonies Earth,
Said the Man of Emeralds dancing in the Spring.
The highest notes from the high heaven descend,
And in the ground notes rise—
The ample grandeur of the Earth, and death and birth
Of seasons . . . all the revolutions of high heaven,
With no confusion.
The small and great complete each other, and the end
Leads to the beginning, and the beginning
Leads to the end, said the Man of Emeralds
Dancing like a wave beneath the bough of Spring.

DATE DU